the guide to owning an
African Grey Parrot

David E. Boruchowitz

Distributed in the UNITED STATES to the Pet Trade by T.F.H. Publications, Inc., 1 TFH Plaza, Neptune City, NJ 07753; on the Internet at www.tfh.com; in CANADA by Rolf C. Hagen Inc., 3225 Sartelon St., Montreal, Quebec H4R 1E8; Pet Trade by H & L Pet Supplies Inc., 27 Kingston Crescent, Kitchener, Ontario N2B 2T6; in ENGLAND by T.F.H. Publications, PO Box 74, Havant PO9 5TT; in AUSTRALIA AND THE SOUTH PACIFIC by T.F.H. (Australia), Pty. Ltd., Box 149, Brookvale 2100 N.S.W., Australia; in NEW ZEALAND by Brooklands Aquarium Ltd., 5 McGiven Drive, New Plymouth, RD1 New Zealand; in SOUTH AFRICA by Rolf C. Hagen S.A. (PTY.) LTD., P.O. Box 201199, Durban North 4016, South Africa; in Japan by T.F.H. Publications. Published by T.F.H. Publications, Inc.

Contents

Introduction

The African Grey (*Psittacus erithacus*) is a beautiful and intelligent parrot that has been popular throughout the ages.

This book takes a notably different approach from that of most pet-care books, but then, an African Grey is a notably different pet. Perhaps the most striking difference between a parrot and most other pets is intelligence, and Greys are perhaps the most intelligent parrots of all. If you think "birdbrain" is an insult and that "to parrot" means to mimic mindlessly, you are in for a big surprise— but a wonderful one.

An African Grey parrot is a fascinating animal friend to have, but bringing one into your home is a little like adopting a perpetual toddler. A Grey will live as long or longer than a human, but it will never go beyond the search-and-destroy stage of a two year old. On the other hand, it will also never outgrow the snugly devotion to you and the need for attention and cuddling that a toddler also shows. So, if you call that stage in human development the "terrible two's," you should consider parrot ownership very carefully. If, however, you call it the "terrific two's," you may just be the right match for an inquisitive, intelligent, and irascible African Grey.

If you are up to this commitment and this challenge, then the first step in accepting the responsibility of African Grey ownership is to learn all you can about these wonderful animals, and this book is the perfect place to start.

We'll first examine the responsibilities of owning a Grey, then we'll look at the parrot in its natural environment and in its long association with humans as a companion animal of a very special kind. Later chapters deal with the details of the basic care and training of your parrot. And a final section finishes the book with a discussion of situations in which there is more than one parrot in a household.

THE COMMITMENT

Owning an African Grey is a much more serious commitment than owning just about any other pet. Yes, there are plenty of pets that cost more to purchase, and almost any dog or horse will cost more to feed and care for. But adding a parrot to your family is just that—adding a family member.

In the wild, a parrot leaves its nest and joins a flock. Its mother and father continue to feed it and watch out for it, and they actively teach it things, from where to find food to how to survive the hazards of their environment. It watches carefully and imitates. Vocalizations are

Because of their extraordinary intelligence, African Greys require a great deal of stimulation, from toys and amusements as well as human companionship.

an important part of the way the family and the flock stay together and alert each other to things of interest or importance. The parrot does not exist as an individual but as part of a social group.

This goes way beyond merely finding food and avoiding predators. Parrots spend a lot of time playing, especially young ones. They play with toys by themselves, shredding bark or leaves, manipulating objects, and doing gymnastics in the tree branches. They also play together, games such as tag and hide-and-seek and other things that have no name in our language. Like us,

A parrot relates to its human family members like flockmates, and it will play, communicate, and otherwise interact with them.

parrots enjoy turning routine chores into fun. They love puzzles and challenges, and they often do things not the fastest or easiest way, but the way that is the most fun.

When you take a parrot into your home, you (and your family) become the bird's flock. It looks to you for guidance and training, and it expects you to interact with it. When it wants to play, it expects you to want to play, too, and while it is perfectly capable of learning that sometimes you cannot play, it will require you to set reasonable rules and to make a mutually convenient schedule.

In addition, you must realize that a parrot remains an emotional "baby" for life, in human terms. The uninhibited emotional displays of a two-year-old human are the lifelong behavior of a parrot. In addition, they are much better armed than a toddler is, because they have a beak that can easily shred wood. I have even heard Greys compared to an axe-wielding two-year-old child who flies.

Not surprisingly, most books about parrots are written by parrot lovers, who tend to go on and on about the merits of parrot ownership (which is often considered to be a state of being owned by a parrot). It is important, however, for those contemplating getting a pet parrot to realize that a parrot is not a pretty talking toy, but a living being with very real needs, both physical and emotional. If you are unsure about getting an African Grey, read this book, visit with some Greys at a pet shop or a breeder, and think hard about it. Remember, your parrot could easily outlive you—this is a lifetime commitment. There are already too many abused, neglected, and abandoned birds out there, so please do not add to the problem by making a hasty decision.

THE GREY CHALLENGE

In addition to what I've just said about parrots as pets, African Grey parrots bring special challenges to a relationship with a human family. This is mainly due to their extreme intelligence. With greater intelligence comes a greater potential to become bored, and, lacking sufficient mental stimulation, Greys often become destructive of their environment and of themselves, plucking their own feathers and otherwise mutilating themselves. (Like any intelligent animal, a Grey can also become vicious if abused, though

Greys often become one-person birds and will choose a favorite caretaker with which to bond.

patient compassion can eventually heal such wounds.)

The key here is to prevent problems by providing a suitable environment for your intelligent, curious pet. A stimulating and challenging setting can be provided with toys, games, other interaction with you, time out of its cage, other pets, and even television. Greys quickly get tired of a toy or a game, so change them often and "recycle" the old ones later. Before long, your parrot will be teaching you new tricks as well.

Another very important trait of Greys is that they are often one-person birds, meaning that they will be loving and affectionate with only one person. Their behavior toward other people can range from timid avoidance to belligerent attack. When a baby Grey is adopted by a family and all the family members care for the bird, it sometimes will bond to the entire family, but even in these circumstances the bird may choose a favorite. This relates to their natural habit of foraging in pairs or small groups. Amazon parrots, on the other hand, can occur in huge flocks, sometimes with more than one species, and they tend to be more accepting of everyone, including strangers, though even with these species there is a lot of individual variation.

Are you an African Grey person? Not all parrot lovers are. The tale is told again and again of someone with a varied collection of birds who winds up keeping only Greys, but the same is true for eclectus parrots, cockatoos, macaws, etc. Without a doubt, Greys are well-represented among those parrots that are kept as single pets by people who share their lives fully with their birds, and their particular blend of traits makes them ideally suited for this type of never-in-the-cage interaction. But they are also demanding pets and prone to nervous disorders if they are neglected. There is no substitute for hands-on experience, so if at all possible, spend some time with several Greys. Like people, each Grey has a distinct personality, but they share many general characteristics. Find out if a Grey is for you.

Natural and Unnatural History

The African Grey parrot has a very long history of association with humans. The species has been known for centuries and was named by the father of modern taxonomy, Linnaeus, in the original round of naming. Although its natural habitat is threatened by development, it is still common in the wild, and it has been well established in aviculture since even before there was aviculture.

The stereotypical picture of a sea captain with a Grey parrot on his shoulder comes from the fact that these intelligent, talking birds were a popular rarity, usually available only to those who traveled to their homelands in Africa. Orphaned or nest-robbed chicks were probably hand-raised by local peoples since antiquity, and their popularity as pets has only grown through the years. Their availability today is good, and you will not have to look too hard to find one for sale.

In this part of the book, we'll look at the species in its native setting, and then in detail at the characteristics of Greys in captivity.

Captive-breeding programs have allowed bird enthusiasts to keep African Greys as pets; such programs have reduced pressure on wild populations.

The Congo subspecies (left) has a bright red tail and is slightly larger than the Timneh race (right), which has a maroon tail and darker gray feathers.

THE AFRICANS

Africa's parrots tend to be stocky, short-tailed, intelligent, talkative, with a green base color accented by gray and by various yellows and reds. Although Africa does not have the diversity and profusion of parrot species that is seen in Central and South America or the Australasian region, it is home to some of the most beloved of parrots, including the lovable lovebirds—tiny parrots who think they are full-sized birds. All lovebirds belong to the genus *Agapornis*. The genus *Poicephalus* contains many species, several of which are well represented in aviculture. These are close cousins to the Grey parrots (and many have prominent gray coloration) and include the Emerald or Brownhead parrot, *P. cryptoxanthus*, the Jardine's parrot, *P. guglielmi*; the Senegal parrot, *P. senegalus*; and the Meyer's parrot, *P. meyeri*. There are other African parrot genera, several of which are extinct.

THE GREYS

The African Grey is the only overall gray parrot. It is the only member of its genus. And yet, it epitomizes parrotness for many people. In fact, its generic name *Psittacus* simply means "parrot" in Latin. So, you could say that it is *the* parrot.

There is only one species of Grey, but a couple of subspecies. Even within a described subspecies, there can be considerable variation in individual birds, both in coloration and in size. Basically, they are all about a foot long, overall gray in color, with a red band on the tail.

Most breeders are careful to keep the subspecies separate, but some of the variability in captive birds is likely due to instances of crossbreeding over the generations. The Grey is a highly variable species in the first place, with the Congo and Timneh races being defined by different descriptions, but with many birds falling well within the two extremes. The possible existence of a third subspecies is argued by some biologists and indicates the variability within the natural populations as well.

The Congo African Grey is the larger subspecies, and is about 13 inches long with a red tail band and a black bill. It is typically light gray, almost silver, with dark scalloping on the feathers.

The Timneh runs about 11 inches long, with a brown or maroon tail band, and a bill that has a light-colored upper mandible. The gray coloration tends to be darker than in the Congo.

Is there any difference in their pet quality? No, just in size and color. In personality there is much more variance between any two individual African Greys than there is between the subspecies.

Compared to other parrots, the Grey has a very large head and neck, making it appear a bit top-heavy. To my eye, they have more of a reptilian appearance than other parrots, and this is accentuated by the scalloped feathers, which look a bit like scales. I mean this in a positive sense; their uniqueness adds to their appeal as not just another run-of-the-mill parrot.

The eye changes color with age, and there are minor differences in coloration between the sexes. Experienced Grey breeders can sex birds by appearance with close to perfect accuracy, but even they are sometimes fooled. Because there isn't a difference in pet quality between males and females, there is no reason for you to worry about telling the difference. If it really matters to you to know which sex your bird is, you can have it DNA sexed.

As far as large parrots go, Greys are not that noisy, though that is a relative judgment that would be denied by someone used to the chattering of a

Other African parrots, including the Senegal, share the prominent gray coloring of the Greys, but none are entirely gray.

budgie. Like most birds, Greys will greet the dawn with a vociferous display, and make no mistake, they are able to screech very loudly! A Grey is not a suitable pet for an apartment, or even a private home with very close neighbors who might be disturbed by the parrot's calls. The already large range of natural sounds a Grey can make is quickly supplemented by the sounds it learns to mimic, and the best advice is if you don't want to hear your pet imitating a particular noise. don't let it hear that noise repeatedly! Also peculiar to Greys is their unbirdlike growl, which they produce when threatened or frightened, and which can be quite unnerving the first time you hear it.

INTELLIGENCE

How intelligent are parrots, and African Greys in particular? First, how do we judge intelligence? The so-called IQ tests are principally verbal. We say that someone who does well on tests in school is quite intelligent. But to the smartest parrot, a graduate level exam from Harvard is simply as good as yesterday's newspaper for lining its cage.

With animals other than humans, we often look to their ability to learn things, to do tricks, to figure their way out of mazes or traps. This, however, presents a double-sided problem. First of all, we are defining intelligence in our terms—can the animal do the things we do? This is unfair, because, for example, the cetaceans—whales and

A five-year-old male Congo displays mature eye coloration; Greys less than a year old have a dark iris that turns yellow as it gets older.

THE GUIDE TO OWNING AN AFRICAN GREY PARROT

porpoises—are clearly intelligent, but they lack the physical apparatus to do many of the things we do, like manipulate objects. On the other hand, if an animal is able to do things by instinct that appear to us to be cognitively complex, then we falsely attribute intelligence to them.

ALEX

People have known for a long time that many birds, particularly psittacines and corvids (parrots and crows), can imitate all types of sounds, from the calls of other species to mechanical noises—and even human language. Parrot lovers have known for quite a while that their birds do not simply "parrot" things they hear, they understand them and respond appropriately both in using and in obeying verbal instructions. The anecdotes of bird people, however, hold little credence in the scientific community.

Dr. Irene Pepperberg is an associate professor of ecology and evolutionary biology, associate professor of psychology, and an affiliate in the program in neuroscience at the University of Arizona, and she has changed all that. For two decades she has been working with Alex, an African Grey parrot, in controlled laboratory conditions, and what she has demonstrated has forever changed the way psychologists look at bird intelligence. She has been extremely careful to apply rigorous experimental protocols to all her work with Alex.

A sharp mind and a gentle nature have earned the Grey its place among the most popular parrots of all time.

For example, although Dr. Pepperberg is teaching him to sound out letters, she does not claim he is learning to read. There is no doubt that Alex is able to count, to discriminate shapes and colors, and to communicate these abilities with English words. Shown a tray of shapes and asked to select the blue block, he can—but he doesn't always. He scores correctly more than 80 percent of the time, but on some tests he scores zero, something that would not happen if he were merely guessing.

The explanation is that on certain days he is fed up with the tests and perversely answers every question wrong on purpose. In fact, he often seems to do just that and only responds correctly when getting something he wants is contingent on it. Does that sound familiar, someone doing something only when there's something in it for them? It is important to remember that Alex has been living in the lab and taking tests like this for 20 years. Wouldn't you be bored if you were in the same classroom for that long? In fact, Alex typically does better on tests that are done with objects he has never seen before. What other than boredom could account for the fact that he answers correctly in discriminating sameness and difference in shape, size, material, color, and number when tested with novel objects, but performs less well with old familiars? If parrots are emotional two year olds, they also have like attention

Researchers have dedicated years of study into the learning capacity and speaking skills of African Greys.

THE GUIDE TO OWNING AN AFRICAN GREY PARROT

spans. In other words, Alex either gets things right or he doesn't pay attention or deliberately chooses to answer incorrectly. This gives him an 80 percent grade, but that average hides the fact that he appears to know his stuff perfectly.

Years ago, I read a memorable "interview" with Alex by a newspaper reporter. After showing off for the visiting reporter, Alex became annoyed and stopped answering altogether. He was shown a handful of three keys and asked "How many?" repeatedly, but he just looked around the room. His keeper gave up and left the room, setting Alex down on the table with the keys. As soon as they were alone, the parrot looked at the keys, then looked the reporter in the eye and said, "Three."

Psychologically Speaking

Because the research focusing on Alex has been above repute, it has been spared much of the controversy surrounding other animal communication investigations.

Dr. Pepperberg has incontrovertibly demonstrated that a bird is capable of much more than mere "parroting" of sounds it hears. (This is not limited to speech, because pet Greys will imitate all sorts of sounds, including the vocalizations of other pets, with which they delight in tormenting those animals, and the ringing of phones, which they use to tease or to summon their human friends.) Other animal psychologists have joined the ranks and expanded our knowledge.

One of the things scientists are concerned with is object permanence, a focus of much of the research of the famous Swiss child psychologist, Jean Piaget. Basically, this is the concept that an object continues to exist even when we cannot perceive it, and it is involved in tracking the movements and location of an object hidden from view, as in the classic shell game.

Animals (and children of various ages) clearly have differing abilities in tracking hidden objects. It is clear that a cat chasing a mouse has some sense of "where has that mouse gone?" but it also seems the animal is asking itself "which of these likely mouse-producing holes is going to yield a mouse this time?" African Greys have a very good sense of object permanence, and reading the results of shell game trials with them makes me wonder if I would do as well! Remember that a bird's visual acuity is extremely well developed.

On many criteria, psychologists judge Alex to have the mental capacities of a four or five-year-old child, but, like all parrots, he has the emotional maturity of a two year old. Petulance, tantrums, disobedience, and other types of perverse behavior are typical. It can be quite exasperating at times; just when a pet parrot appears to be on the verge of real dialogue with you, it will become annoyed and insist on taking a bath or throwing a toy at you. To parrot lovers, however, this is part of the charm of the birds; because they do not expect their pets to be five year olds, the fact that they always act like extremely intelligent

The Grey's excellent talking ability sets it apart from most other parrots; the species has an uncanny way of mimicking the tones and inflections of the human voice.

two year olds does not perturb them. This is the key to living with and loving an African Grey—accept the bird for the marvel that it is.

WHERE DOES THAT LEAVE GREYS?

How intelligent is Alex? How intelligent are African Greys? We cannot answer that quantitatively, and we must be careful about a bird's ability to perform tricks that look like reasoning or intelligent use of language. Also, we should not confuse parameters. When someone says that

Alex has a four-year-old child's mental capabilities, this is not meant universally; that is, he has specific abilities equivalent to the four-year-old human, such as object permanence, counting, same-different discrimination, etc. He does not have the linguistic abilities of four-year-old humans, some of whom can converse fluently in several languages, while much of Alex's communication is in single words.

Let's rephrase the question. You show your bird a key ring and ask, "What are these?" The bird answers, "Keys." You then ask, "How many?" The bird tilts its head to look at them and correctly responds, "Two." What does this tell us about the animal?

Perception

Well, for one thing, it tells us that this bird is quite attuned to its environment and able to discriminate objects and to categorize them. This ability, not really demonstrable in a newt, for example, indicates that assessing the bird's quality of life must take into account psychological factors as well as physical ones.

Symbols

It tells us that a Grey can deal symbolically, for all language is symbolic. A dog that learns to sit on command understands symbols, but dogs do not demonstrate the depth of symbol use that the speaking bird does.

Desire

It also tells us that birds have—or can develop—a desire to communicate with us. When a macaw snuggles up to its owner, lavishing kisses upon the person, and says, "I love you!" it is hard to ignore the implications. The same bird might say "Yuck!" and throw down a dish containing a food it doesn't care for. Why? It's not rewarded for the behavior. It doesn't gain it anything. Those who work with these animals, however, know that the bird, like a spoiled child (something parrot owners quickly admit of their charges), is trying to communicate its disgust in the hopes of getting a preferred treat. They want to talk to us, and to listen to us.

The Linguistic Advantage

All of this suggests that the appropriate question isn't one of quantifying a parrot's intelligence, but of trying to understand how its linguistic abilities can be part of an incredible and lifelong bond between you and your pet.

Animal lovers of all kinds will report tales of deep affection and almost telepathic communication between them and their pets—a true two-way bond that goes very deep. I am sure you know of many such cases. My own experience includes a cat that clearly understood the emotional turmoil of her troubled teen owner and who was at times the girl's only confidante and support. I also know of a dog that saved its family by alerting them to a fire in the house—and this particular tale is quite common. With a bird like an African Grey, however, you might have the opportunity to talk with your pet! This is

Toys are essential to the happiness and mental well-being of a Grey; they especially love puzzle games and objects they can take apart.

Though handfed babies can be affectionate and cuddly, some older Greys will shy away from close human contact.

an incredible thing, even if the discussion is by necessity rudimentary. And even if your parrot never speaks itself, it will definitely learn to comprehend your speech to a much greater level than a dog ever could.

This elevates the bond that can form between you and your Grey, and, because the parrot's life span can easily exceed four times a dog's life span, your very special feathered friend can be a friend for life.

Finding a Grey

Logically, this chapter belongs here in the introductory section, but as I mentioned in the previous chapter, you need to know a lot about these birds before deciding if you should get one. Please read the entire book before you even think of looking for a pet Grey.

CAPTIVE-BRED OR WILD-CAUGHT?

The following recommendation is guaranteed to be controversial: do not buy a wild-caught parrot. That statement will anger only two types of people, however—exporters/importers and people who know a wild-caught African Grey that is an ideal pet. There is no doubt that a wild-caught bird can make a wonderful companion. There is, however, ample reason why wild birds should not be trapped and sold, except for specialized breeding programs concerned with genetic diversity.

That leaves captive-bred birds, of which there are many, because Greys usually breed readily in captivity when given the proper conditions. There are two types of captive-bred birds available—parent-raised and handfed.

Parent-Raised Birds

Parent-raised birds are hatched and reared in aviaries or cages, but they are incubated and fed by their parents until they are weaned (eating food on their own). These birds are less expensive than handraised birds, for obvious reasons. They have some natural fear of people and are socialized as parrots, even though they are used to these funny mammals that come around offering tasty food every day.

Can such birds make good pets? That depends. They are, of course, no less intelligent or playful than handfed parrots. A great many of them become superlative talkers, too. In fact, Alex, Dr. Irene Pepperberg's famous talking Grey, is

Mature birds make fine pets, but most new owners still choose to begin with a young bird.

not a hand-raised bird. And like Alex, some even become tame, allowing you to handle them and perching on your shoulder or arm. Often, however, they do not bond with people in the way that handfed birds do, acting as if they and we are all one big flock and family. Because a Grey is so intelligent, it will readily learn that you are a kind provider, and if it is your only bird, it will depend on you for the social interaction that is so important to these parrots. You are several steps ahead, however, if you start with a handfed bird.

I have seen parent-raised parrots that were much tamer and friendlier than handfed birds that did not get the proper attention after weaning. In fact, sometimes a handfed bird that simply gets placed into a cage after weaning and is not adopted into a home becomes much nippier than parent-raised birds. This is because the parrot fails to bond permanently with people, so it has no fear of (or respect for) us!

I once visited a major breeder of all types of parrots, from cockatiels to cockatoos, and I asked her about using handfed pets as breeders. She replied that she had many such birds, and they were extremely dangerous during breeding season. Because they have no fear of humans, they attack savagely and uninhibitedly when she inspects the nest boxes. Interestingly, when they are not breeding, these birds are usually sweet and loving, which demonstrates the power of hormones and instinct!

Handfed

Hand-raised birds are either hatched in incubators or taken from their parents at a very early age and fed by hand. This is an extremely time-consuming activity, and it requires a lot of knowledge, equipment, and patience. Birds needing to be fed every two hours do not care about work schedules, television shows, or your need for sleep. They can and do get sick, need veterinary care, and sometimes die, taking the investment of time and money with them. Therefore, hand-raised birds are much more expensive than parent-raised ones, often costing twice as much. Is it worth it?

For many, the answer to that is an emphatic "Yes!" Handfed parrots think they are people, or at least that we are funny-looking flightless birds. As juveniles they are eager to find that special person or family who will take them into their home. Years ago I visited a large pet shop that had an open display of a half dozen baby Greys. My young son walked over to get a closer look, and the next thing he knew he had parrots on both arms and shoulders. The little guys latched onto his nearest sleeve and climbed up, clamoring for attention. Each one of the inquisitive and affectionate birds made a protest when removed—and it was awfully hard to get my son away, too!

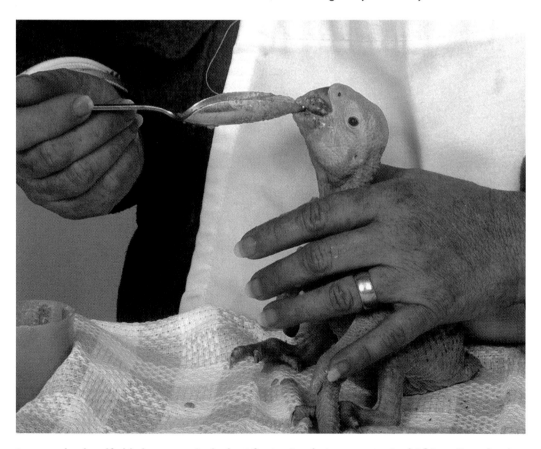

In general, a handfed baby parrot is the best for taming, but a parent-raised African Grey that has been properly socialized can prove just as tame.

PET STORE OR BREEDER?

I often hear people slam pet shops and extol breeders as sources for pet birds. This, however, is a gross oversimplification. There are superlative pet retailers who sell fantastic pet parrots, and there are horrible breeders who sell diseased birds to unsuspecting buyers. As in any business transaction, and especially as in any transaction involving live animals, it is vital to know the person or firm with which you are dealing. The two-edged sword here is that some pet shop employees have no real knowledge or experience, and some breeders use their private status to hide a multitude of sins.

The Breeder Advantage

Someone who breeds parrots has to know a lot about them. If they also handfeed babies, they have to know even more. No breeder will succeed if they simply hire high school kids without extensive training to come in and care for their birds. Pet shops, however, sometimes have such unskilled staff, and their "advice" can be dismal indeed.

In addition, most breeders I have met are caring, dedicated people who admit that they are lucky if their "business" brings in enough money to cover expenses. Most people raising parrots do it because they enjoy it, not because it makes them rich—it doesn't!

This means that a breeder has intimate knowledge of the birds for sale. A Grey purchased from a breeder may come with a name, a hatch certificate, photos, favorite toys—in other words, it is more like an adoption than a purchase. After the sale, the breeder is typically available for advice, and many take emergency phone calls 24 hours a day, seven days a week.

The Retailer Advantage

Pet stores operate on a very small profit margin, and the sale of livestock rarely keeps them in business. A pet owner, therefore, is much more valuable as a customer than as a sale. By that I mean that their foremost concern is making sure you are happy with your purchases so you will come back for other pets and supplies. Your satisfaction or lack thereof would be unlikely to affect a private breeder in the same way, though many care deeply in any case.

It is easy to find out how long a pet shop has been in business and to get people's opinion of it. You can visit it regularly and see how all of the animals are cared for over time. It is much harder to get this information about a breeder, especially one who operates a tightly closed aviary. Many breeders refuse to allow visitors into their breeding facilities for extremely good reasons. But if you don't know anything about them, how can you tell if they are simply trying to hide a substandard operation?

Your Choice

Knowing your particular source is much more important than whether that source is a retail establishment or a private breeder. When we are talking about the sale of birds in the $500 to $1,000 range, it is obvious that no supplier of any kind will

THE GUIDE TO OWNING AN AFRICAN GREY PARROT

survive long in business if they do not properly care for their animals.

Recommendations are always a help, so if you know someone who has bought a Grey or other parrot, find out where they got it. Ask for a recommendation on pertinent Internet forums. A little bit of research can pay off enormously.

Ask plenty of questions. It will rapidly become clear if the person you are talking to knows anything about birds, and about the bird in question in particular. Let's look at four extreme cases to see the benefits of such questioning:

1. Disreputable Store

"This bird? It's an African Grey. Nine hundred bucks—great talker!"

"How many words does it say?"

"I think it says 'hello,' and something else. But that's because it's a baby. When it gets older it'll be able to answer the phone for you."

"How old is it?"

"Uh, I'd have to look that up, but not too old."

"What is it eating?"

"Bird seed."

"Just seed?"

"Well, Joe usually feeds the birds. I do fish."

"Is Joe available?"

"Nah, he's off today."

"I see. Is the bird handfed?"

"No, it eats all by itself."

"I meant, was it handfed? Is it tame?"

"Oh, sure! It bit Joe the other day, but that's because he didn't like being picked up."

"So Joe would be the one to see if I have any questions after I bring the bird home?"

"Yeah, I guess. He's been here the longest—about six months, I think. He's in on Tuesdays and Thursdays, and he sometimes closes on Saturday."

2. Disreputable Breeder

"This bird? It's an African Grey. I sell a lot of these—they're great talkers!"

"How many words does it say?"

"Most of my babies say 'up' and "hello.' They don't really start talking until they're older."

"How old is it?"

"Well, I'd have to check the records to be sure, but he's fully weaned."

"What is it eating?"

"I feed Acme brand pellets—it's all a bird needs."

"Just pellets?"

"Well, sometimes I give 'em a treat, you know, like peanuts."

"Is the bird handfed?"

"Yes. I pull all my babies at about two weeks and handfeed them."

"What if I have questions or problems? Can I call you?"

"Sure. I'm usually here. If not, leave a message on the machine, and I'll get back to you. But there's really no trick to these birds—just feed 'em and clean the cage."

3. Reputable Store

"This bird? It's an African Grey. One of the best talkers among the parrots, though each bird is different."

"How many words does it say?"

"It doesn't speak yet, but it knows the

step up command, and I heard it whistling yesterday."

"How old is it?"

"Uh, let me see...it was hatched on June third."

"What is it eating?"

"I feed a pellet-seed mixture, with fresh fruits and vegetables, and occasional treats."

"Can I feed it just seed?"

"No, it needs a balanced diet, just like you."

"I see. Is the bird handfed?"

"Definitely. I only buy from the most reputable breeders, and I finish handfeeding them here in the store. I can show you two Greys I'm feeding right now."

"What if I have questions or problems? Can I call you?"

"Here's a card with our store hours on them. Ask either for me or for Sally—she's the girl who helps me with birds. And here's a card with the number of a good avian vet in the community, and an emergency after-hours number."

4. Reputable Breeder

"This bird? It's an African Grey named Paco, one of Gretchen and Sam's chicks. They always produce my biggest chicks. This one has been consistently 20 to 50 grams heavier than the others his own age."

"'His'?"

"Well, I haven't had him DNA'd, but I'm right 95 percent of the time."

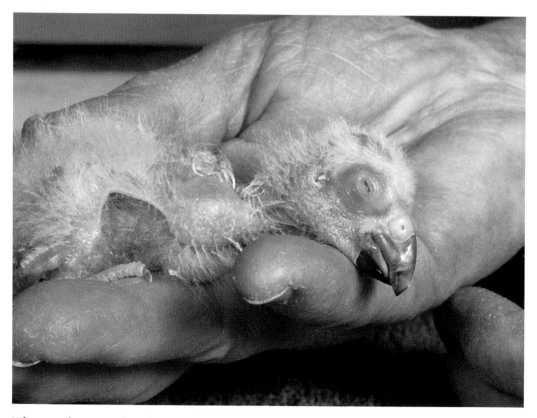

Whatever the source, breeder or pet store, a health guarantee is something that should be discussed when obtaining a new bird.

THE GUIDE TO OWNING AN AFRICAN GREY PARROT

"How many words does he say?"

"Greys don't usually talk as babies, though I have had a couple that did. This guy has been making a sound that might be 'up,' but it's too early to tell. He will step up on command, though. Look... Paco? Up!"

"Hey! That's great. How old is he?"

"This baby was one of my March chicks...let's see...March ninth."

"What is it eating?"

"I feed all my birds a home-cooked bean and rice mixture, and I supplement with a little seed, some pellets, and plenty of fresh produce—I try to feed six to ten different types per day. I also make birdie bread for them three times a week."

"I see. So you handfed this one?"

"I handfeed all my babies from day one, unless I'm raising them for breeders. This little guy has been a real sweetie, though he scared me when he was about a month old. I thought he was getting an impacted crop, but he had just overeaten a bit. I cut the little piglet back a few cc's per feeding, and he was fine. You have to watch him, though, he'll beg for pizza till it breaks your heart, but a tiny taste is all you should give him."

"What if I have questions or problems? Can I call you?"

"Yes, day or night. I want you and Paco to be perfectly happy."

Get the idea? Whether store or breeder, the best ways to locate a source for your Grey are by word of mouth, through magazine and newspaper ads, and on Internet sites and lists.

Happy Housing

A secure and pleasant cage must be provided for a new parrot; it will need a place for shelter and rest.

Many African Greys have pretty much free run of their humans' homes. Your house can be your Grey's house, too, but only if certain requirements are met. The bird should never be allowed unsupervised liberty; there is too much damage it can do and too much danger that can threaten its safety. And even if the door is never closed, your pet must have a cage of its own—a place where it knows it can rest in safety and security.

A huge variety of cages are available on the market, and many types of homemade cages are equally serviceable. If you choose to make your own cage, you must study proper cage construction, either by reading about it or by talking with a breeder who makes cages. These details are outside the scope of this book. A cage can be made quite easily from welded wire with connecting J-clips, but you must make sure that the cage is suitable and safe for your bird. Aside from

Play gyms can either be fitted to the top of a cage or moved to different locations—either way, they are great for exercise and fun.

the cage size and shape, you must keep in mind such factors as mesh spacing, wire gauge, and the dangers of zinc poisoning, which we'll discuss in a later chapter.

A REFUGE CAGE

The parrot that is free all or most of the time has minimal needs in a cage, and a 24-inch cube might suffice. Because even birds given total liberty should be locked in at night, the cage will serve at least as a sleeping roost. The cage must be of adequate size that the bird can freely flap its wings (fly in place), with bar spacing such that it cannot get its head wedged between the bars. It should have at least one sturdy perch, plus food and water utensils, and room for some toys.

A HOME CAGE

When a bird is confined to its cage part of the time, the cage must be considerably bigger. How big? That is a controversial topic, and the answer partly depends on the amount of time the bird will be spending in the cage. I would hate to see a Grey confined in any cage less than 3 or 4 feet long, and larger would be much better. If the bird is full-flighted (we'll discuss wing clipping in the next chapter), a flight or aviary 8 feet long will allow it proper exercise. On the other hand, if the bird is allowed to fly around the house part of the day, this is not a necessity. Although aesthetic concerns typically produce cages that are tall vertically, it is horizontal flight space that is important for your bird's exercise. In the event that your bird will be kept in the cage for long periods (days at a time), it is important to give it as much room as possible, both for exercise and to allow room for the toys that are vital to a solitary parrot's well-being.

A PLAY GYM

Many parrots spend a lot of time on a play gym, and this is an excellent way to provide for your pet while still allowing it freedom from its cage and the ability to interact with its human family. A gym can be bought or homemade, and as simple as a section of branched tree trunk fixed securely in an upright position on which you hang toys, or as complex as a maze of PVC ladders, perches, and swings, complete with hanging chains, ropes, built-in feed and water dishes, and a removable dropping pan under the whole thing. Some parrot aficionados who own more than one bird have gigantic gyms on which all their pets can play at the same time.

Because much of a parrot's natural movement is through feet-over-beak-over-feet climbing, it is important that your bird's gym have several inter-connected levels, and it will enjoy ladders, tightropes, and bridges, whether natural branches or plastic, wood, or metal substitutes. Make sure that all

If your pet store allows it, try taking your Grey in to pick out its own toys.

THE GUIDE TO OWNING AN AFRICAN GREY PARROT

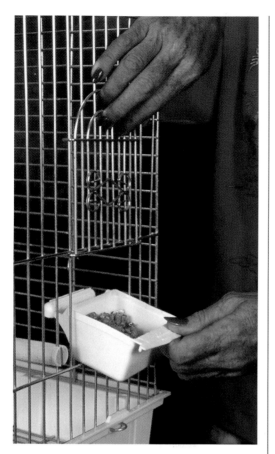

When choosing a cage, consider ease of access and cleanup. It's much easier to change food and water dishes from the outside of a cage than the inside.

materials used in the gym are safe for your bird to chew on.

BATHING

Almost all parrots love to bathe, and many parrot owners enjoy having their pets join them in the shower. If this does not appeal to you, you can give the bird a shower of its own—there are even PVC shower perches available that attach to the tile with suction cups. Or, you can let your pet bathe in a large basin of lukewarm water. Remember that bathing is good for your bird, but shampoos or soaps should only be used in the rare event that the bird gets greasy dirt on it, because they remove the natural oils that are important for feather condition. Always make sure your Grey has a warm, draft-free place to preen until its feathers are completely dry, and never allow it to bathe just before bedtime.

An African Grey will appreciate the fresh air and sunlight when its cage is placed near a window; however, be certain that your bird won't get overheated or chilled.

Living With a Grey

We must not forget in all this discussion of talking and puzzle solving and temper tantrums that a parrot has physical needs

Toys are great fun, but a shy or hesitant Grey may need some time to get used to a new object.

as well. There are a number of considerations that will help you meet those needs and keep your pet happy and healthy.

HANDLING

The first key to handling a parrot is that you need the bird's cooperation. With the exception of restraint for grooming or medical procedures, you should always provide the opportunity and let the bird come to you. A properly weaned baby should know to step up on command when you hold out your hand to it. Once on your hand, it might continue up your arm and onto your head or shoulder, or you might bring it close to your face for one-on-one talking and birdie kisses.

Many parrots love to cuddle, being cradled on their backs in your arms like a baby. Others prefer to be scratched and petted while standing next to you. Almost all tame birds will give kisses, because this behavior is very similar to their natural feeding behaviors. In fact, do not be surprised or (alarmed) if your Grey regurgitates "presents" for you.

WING CLIPPING

To clip or not to clip? There are two diametrically opposed schools of thought. The first is dominated by the idea that a bird is meant to fly, and clipping wing feathers to prevent flight is unnatural and mean. There is no doubt that Greys are superb and powerful flyers, and their grace and beauty while in flight are augmented by the obvious joy they have in being able to defy gravity in a way we humans can only dream of.

On the other hand, clipped birds appear to be quite happy, ambling around and climbing wherever they want to go. And, obviously, they cannot fly away. Is this a concern? Most definitely! There are many remorseful people who swear, "I will never keep an unclipped bird again!"

But will a tame bird, bonded to you and your family, just fly the coop? Well, yes and no. Such a bird is unlikely to make an escape to get away from you, but it is quite likely to take advantage of an open

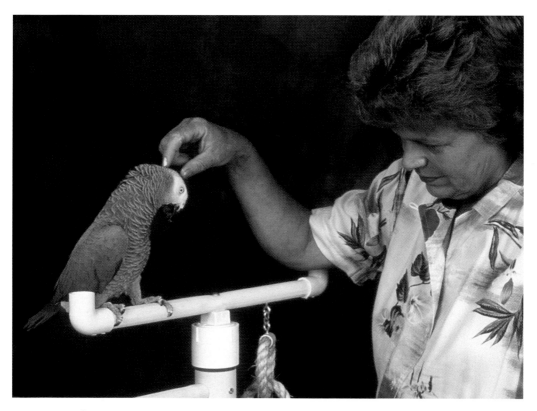

Never try to force contact on your bird—only when a bird is willing should you approach.

Whether or not to wing clip is an owner's choice; but don't attempt to do it without first watching someone with experience.

door or window or an unlatched cage to follow its natural instincts and take to the skies. The problem is that a bird raised indoors in captivity does not learn to take note of landmarks, or how to navigate. It explodes from a house and finds itself in a dazzling and bewildering environment. Only a few powerful wingbeats might take it farther than it's ever flown before, hundreds of feet into the open sky, from which your house is only a tiny roof far below. Never having seen the roof, it has no reason to associate it with you or your home. A bus snorting by, an airplane, or even a flock of crows can spook the poor parrot, sending it in a headlong flight that

may take it right out of the neighborhood. Before the bird even thinks about heading home, it may be so lost that it has no hope of return.

Are lost Greys ever reunited with their families? Yes. A few lucky ones that aren't stolen, or killed, or frightened so far away that the owners never think of advertising their loss in that location make it back. I recently read of a found Grey in California that was claimed by hundreds of people wanting to cash in on a free pet parrot. The correct owner was finally identified when the bird spoke to her—in both English and Russian—as she had claimed her bird could.

TATTOOING AND MICROCHIPPING

Potential theft or loss makes permanently identifying your parrot important. A bird that has been surgically sexed will also have been tattooed, and many birds are microchipped. In this simple procedure a chip is injected under the skin and can be read by a microchip reader at any time in the future to prove identity and ownership. Your vet should be able to perform either procedure for you.

NAIL CLIPPING

The best way to clip your parrot's nails is to provide plenty of different sized perches, including some concrete or lava stone ones, so that the nails are worn down naturally. If they get too long anyway, clipping them is no different from cutting a dog's or cat's nails, and a hand-tame bird is usually cooperative.

A bird should be properly restrained in a towel before you try to clip its nails. Again, seek the assistance of someone with experience.

Wrapping the bird in a towel prevents thrashing of the wings and possible injury to your pet, while a helper to hold the bird's head and keep and eye on the beak is a good idea to prevent injury to you. Be careful not to trim too far, but if the nail bleeds, a little styptic powder will stop it quickly.

BEAK TRIMMING

Parrots that have access to various gnawing toys and materials rarely have a problem with overgrown beaks, but some birds are simply prone to uneven growth and wind up needing a trim. It is not difficult to do, but the safest way is to have your veterinarian do it the first time and show you how. Keeping plenty of gnawing toys around will help prevent the problem.

TAMING

A handfed baby does not need taming in the sense that it already has no fear of people and is used to being handled. It will, however, need time to adjust to you and your home. Remember that patience and kindness always work with a parrot, and frustration and anger are always counterproductive. The most effective punishment for a parrot is to be ignored, and attention is the greatest reward. This

The step up command is one of the first things to work on when taming and training. From there, you may move on to more commands and, eventually, tricks.

Grooming does not have to be traumatic. Here, a Timneh Grey enjoys a foot massage after its routine nail trim.

means that if your bird begins shrieking for attention, and you give it attention, you have just rewarded it for making a raucous commotion. Instead, a stern "No!" and a few minutes of being ignored will demonstrate the inappropriateness of the behavior.

TRAINING

There will be things other than "step up" and "no!" that you will want to teach your pet, such as how to behave at the table, where in your home it is and is not allowed, etc. You can expect it to learn such things, but you can also expect it to be about as obedient as a two-year-old child—sometimes temptation is too great for even the best of intentions.

As far as tricks are concerned, your parrot will be capable of learning very complex routines, as long as you practice patience and rely on reward rather than punishment to teach it. By breaking a complex behavior into a series of simple behaviors you can get your bird to do just about anything it is physically capable of. (Sunflower seeds make great reinforcers.)

MOODS

You get moody, I get moody—we all do. And so do Greys. Sometimes they just don't feel like cooperating, or cuddling, or eating, or whatever it is you want them to do. Respect your bird's individuality and personal preferences and give it space when it wants to be alone. On the other hand, your parrot will also have periods of joyous glee,

"Step up" is the foundation for more complicated routines. It also helps with day-to-day maneuvers such as cage cleaning and grooming.

when it wants to play or joke around and won't take no for an answer. You should never be too busy for this kind of fun.

SEX

The sex of your bird should have little bearing on its life as a pet. It can, however, have a large effect on its life as a bird. Greys, like many parrots, form very stable pair bonds, and it is not uncommon for a handfed pet to become partially romantically attached to a human. Usually this means you will get a lot of feeding from your bird, but sometimes a passionate parrot can also become very aggressive and nippy, especially toward people it sees as rivals for your affection.

Fortunately, Greys are less likely to behave this way than many other large parrot species. Occasionally, a pet parrot reaching sexual maturity (about 5 to 10 years, depending on species) becomes so intractable that it must be placed into a breeding situation instead, but Greys are not the usual culprits.

A MULTI-BIRD HOUSEHOLD

We've been concentrating on keeping a single Grey as a pet. In these last two short chapters of the book, we'll look at some of the issues involved in keeping more than one bird. This can be a home with more than one pet Grey, or one Grey with other species of parrots. But perhaps we should first quickly consider a Grey as the only bird in a multi-pet household.

Greys and Other Pets

Many parrot owners make the mistake of treating not only their parrot, but also their other pets as little feathered or furred people. I do not care how domesticated and imprinted and bonded an animal is, it still has instincts. And, although many dogs wouldn't stand a chance against a parrot's beak, there are many other dogs—not all of them large ones—that can dispatch a large parrot with a quick shake to break its neck.

Stick a pin into a dog, and it will turn to bite. True, many will stop short of puncturing your hand with their teeth,

A household with more than one bird means that the birds will be more likely to entertain themselves; on the other hand, they may be less inclined to bond with humans.

THE GUIDE TO OWNING AN AFRICAN GREY PARROT

Greys can do well in situations with other species; however, it's always a good idea for each bird to have its own refuge cage.

but that is because learning takes over from the instinct. Despite what it may seem, your dog does not share your love for your parrot, and there is little reason to believe it will check its bite if the parrot is the one causing it pain. To be fair, a parrot has the ability to maim or kill a dog or cat as well, and given the right circumstances, it will.

So, am I saying you can't have these pets together? Absolutely not, and many people enjoy veritable menageries in their homes. The successful ones, however, will rely on observation and careful supervision, not on some nebulous we're-all-one-big-happy-family philosophy. Every animal has its own traits and its own perceptions, and recognizing and understanding this is central to having animals of different species get along with each other.

For example, I know of a boxer that was a killing machine. It killed woodchucks, poultry, cats—even raccoons. The farm on which it lived had a public road dividing the house area from the barn area. The barn cats were tolerated anywhere on the property, as long as they were on the far

If breeding is a consideration, a viable pair must be established; however, compatibility does not guarantee breeding success.

THE GUIDE TO OWNING AN AFRICAN GREY PARROT

side of the road. If they ventured across the road toward the house, they were in touble. But, the house cats were tolerated anywhere—more than tolerated, for the kittens would climb all over the dog and bat at his ears while he dozed. He arrived at these "rules" totally on his own, and it was never clear how he knew which cats were which.

So, can dogs and cats and rabbits and monkeys and horses and pot-bellied pigs and African Greys coexist peacefully? Yes, perhaps. But be careful. Introduce the animals as young as possible. Be careful not to let them get jealous of the attention you give. And always keep an eye on things. Remember that the primary driving force in nature is predation, and that animals don't need something to be on a plate to consider it food.

Other Birds

It shouldn't surprise you to learn that parrots in general and Greys in particular can be very jealous and possessive. Even when they are pals, pet parrots will always be vying for more attention, the choicest treats, the best toys.

On the other hand, like a barrel of monkeys, a group of parrots provides a gestalt much greater than their individual contributions, and the birds serve as playmates for each other, lessening the burden on you to interact with them socially. Thus, it is a trade-off between the increased dynamics of the group and the decreased requirements of each bird.

A very good comparison is with parents of multiple birth children. Twins

or triplets or quadruplets are, in many ways, much more than two or three or four times the work of a single baby, but their parents will also tell you that the cumulative effects extend to the positive benefits as well as the chores. And, while most human parents don't get to choose whether they will learn about multiple newborns firsthand, African Grey owners can usually decide in advance what type of relationship they want with their pet birds.

Three Shades of Grey

There are basically three types of Grey-owner relationships.

Only Child

The scenario in which a Grey is the only bird in the household—and often the only pet—is most often the result of someone discovering the charms of a Grey and becoming a bird owner because of falling in love with these magnificent animals. Like parents of an only child, they dote on their parrots, and the bond between them is very personal and intense. Many consider this the ultimate relationship, and it is, but only in the sense that it maximizes the human element of it. That is, the parrot becomes a member of the family in the maximum sense.

Exclusively Greys

Starting with one Grey or with a group of mixed parrot species, a person sometimes becomes so captivated by the charms of African Grey parrots that they come to surround themselves with these birds. Some take the breeding route, maintaining perhaps dozens of breeding pairs in vast aviaries. These people are not immune to the appeal of an intimate human-Grey relationship, and they sometimes even have a single personal pet Grey, but they focus instead on the natural appeal of these birds, and on reproducing them so that other people can learn the joys of being owned by an African Grey. Others create a collection of tame pet Greys—the nursery school approach in which their homes are always full of mischief and wonder.

Greys in a Rainbow

This third type of Grey owner also comes in two varieties. The first has an aviary full of all different species of birds, including Greys. These people appreciate the natural charm of Greys as part of a rainbow of appeal. The second runs a rainbow-colored daycare center, with pet parrots of all types interacting with each other and with their humans as only a mixed group of parrots can—one step this side of pandemonium and insanity, but those who choose this route claim it is also one step short of paradise

Preparation

I think you can see that central to all these Grey-human relationships is a knowledge of and familiarity with these birds. Because you are reading this book, you are unlikely to have that experience already, and the way to get it is with a pet Grey. Although some Grey owners did not start with a single pet, it is perhaps the best way to go.

Feeding and Nutrition

What does a healthy African Grey eat? What doesn't a healthy African Grey eat! When a Grey (or any parrot for that matter) is properly raised, it will be weaned to a huge variety of foods, concentrating on grains, legumes, commercial pellets, fruits, and vegetables. The most successful parrot breeders feed many different items, and many do not feed any seed at all. This is not because seed is in itself bad, but because birds can develop the bad habit of refusing anything but seed, which by itself is not an adequate diet. Seeds are notably deficient in vitamins, minerals, and certain proteins.

Because Greys are so curious, it is likely that your pet will want to sample anything that you eat. This can be fine, as long as your own eating habits are exemplary. Foods that are bad for us, like salt, concentrated sweets, and fats, are also not good for your bird, and some can

be downright dangerous or even lethal. In this chapter we will outline a proper diet for a pet parrot—something that is very much mix and match in nature.

Greys enjoy a wide range of foods. Help stimulate your bird by making mealtime an adventure, not a predictable chore.

A manageable chunk of fresh corn is a nutritious treat that your Grey can enjoy devouring.

ESSENTIAL NUTRIENTS

All animals need certain nutrients to thrive. The exact nutritional requirements of parrots have not been researched as they have for humans, but in the last few decades enormous progress has been made in determining their needs. The surprising finding was that their needs are quite like our own.

Protein

Protein is the building block of the cell. It is the stuff of which muscles are made, and it is used in the genetic direction of all life functions. Different proteins are made up of a variety of amino acids, and these amino acids are found in varying amounts in different food items. The basic distinction is between animal protein and plant protein.

For many herbivorous species, this distinction is irrelevant. They are able to take plant protein and turn it into their own (animal) protein. Omnivores and carnivores, however, often cannot synthesize enough amino acids to survive on plant protein alone, and they need animal protein in their diet as well. People and parrots are in this group, though it is possible to meet our protein needs by very carefully combining different plant proteins. Nutrients such as B vitamins, however, are still lacking in such a diet, sometimes referred to as a macrobiotic diet.

So, the bulk of your Grey's protein should come from vegetable sources such as grains, seeds (including legumes like peas and beans), and nuts. Some animal protein in the form of cooked lean meat or eggs is also good. Some parrots also like a bit of cooked fish.

Carbohydrates

Carbohydrates (sugars and starches) are energy sources, and the best sources of these for your parrot are fruits, grains, and seeds (including legumes such as peas and beans). This should immediately give you the hint that grains and seeds can make up a major portion of your bird's diet and provide both protein and carbohydrates.

Simple sugars in high concentrations lead to obesity and other medical problems. Though it is unlikely that you will overfeed fresh fruits to that extent, if you feed your parrot many sweetened treats (as in candy) or naturally concentrated sugars (as in raisins), it amounts to parrot "junk food."

Fats

Fats are necessary in the diet to provide concentrated energy reserves and also as a source of certain vitamins. Because they are the most efficient way of storing fuel, it is also very easy to overindulge. Whether human or psittacine, a couch potato lifestyle leads to obesity, liver problems, and other ailments. Although some parrots such as Hyacinth macaws have a high-fat diet because they feed primarily on oil-rich nuts, a Grey's natural diet is not particularly high in fat, and the relatively sedentary habits of a pet Grey requires you to limit its intake of fatty foods. These include nuts, oily seeds such

Though seeds should not make up a major portion of your Grey's diet, they can be included with nuts and dried fruits as part of a treat.

as sunflower, fried foods, and other great-tasting, greasy, bad-for-you treats.

Vitamins

These substances were originally labeled "vital amines" because of their absolute necessity for life, even though they are required only in minute quantities. In fact, many vitamins are poisonous in any appreciable amounts. This means that natural vitamin sources are preferable over artificial supplements, and you must be careful about using supplements cumulatively—for example,

WARNING
Chocolate, not a desirable food for any species, can be fatal to birds in very small amounts. If you indulge, don't share your chocolate with your pet.

Spray millet is a delicacy for most parrots, including Greys; large sprays can be clipped to a cage for easy access.

a liquid vitamin supplement with vitamin-enriched pellets.

The number one source for vitamins is fresh fruits and vegetables, though they are found in all types of foods. Vitamin A is especially important for birds, and it is abundant in dark green and yellow vegetables, which are also tasty treats for your parrot.

MINERALS

Minerals are metallic nutrients such as calcium, magnesium, and phosphorus, which are essential for bone growth, egg production, the proper functioning of the nervous system, and other bodily functions. They are especially crucial in the diet of breeding birds—for the female to produce eggshells and for both sexes to provide enough minerals for the proper growth of the chicks.

Biological sources of minerals are, not surprisingly, bones and eggshells. Most parrots enjoy chewing on bones, and eggshells are easily crushed and added to a variety of food. Oyster shell, available at feed stores, can also be offered. Cuttlebone, the mantle (inner shell) of cuttlefish (squid), has long been a popular mineral source for pet birds. Because it is so soft, however, a Grey can reduce it to dust in a matter of minutes, in which case its actual consumption of the nutrients is probably negligible. Cuttlebone can, however, be scraped into or onto soft foods to supplement their mineral content.

Natural gypsum rock, limestone, and other stones can also provide minerals for your bird. These provide the additional benefit of being good for keeping the bird's beak in proper trim.

I have seen photos of a huge flock of macaws that makes a daily stop at a mud cliff, where the birds ingest clay they scrape off the cliffside. The biologists studying this behavior were not sure what minerals the birds were seeking, but it obviously fulfilled some need.

Years ago people would throw a chunk of old plaster into their parrot's cage as a mineral supplement. The problem with this practice is that old plaster chunks often contain old paint, which means lead poisoning. In addition, it's hard to find plaster today—old or otherwise. Fortunately, there are available manufactured mineral blocks that are even better than plain plaster. Some birds will whittle these down to a pile of dust as soon as they get them, in which case the blocks should be scraped onto soft foods instead of being hung in the cage. Most birds, however, will simply nibble on them from time to time.

Trace Elements

It is in the field of trace elements that many dietary deficiencies become manifest. Trace elements are nutrients needed in very small amounts, and often these become very dangerous at levels much above that. Examples are zinc, iodine, selenium, and molybdenum. Supplementation of trace elements, whether for yourself or for your pet is a risky practice and should never be done except under medical supervision. A deficiency in them, however, leads to poor health, breeding problems, and even premature death. For example, veterinarians in different parts of the country, where natural selenium levels in the soil can differ widely, might see animals with selenium deficiency or "white muscle disease," or animals with symptoms of selenium toxicity. So, what do you do?

Liquid vitamins may be added to your bird's water if necessary; however, treated water tends to foul very quickly and must be changed frequently.

You normally cannot overdose with natural sources of trace elements. Even a given foodstuff—say grapes—will vary a great deal from batch to batch in the trace elements it contains, and the exact amounts needed are not known and vary from species to species and probably even from individual to individual, so the best diet is one that contains the widest variety of foodstuffs. Instead of always feeding spinach, for example, alternate with kale, chard, carrot tops, dandelion leaves, etc. Rotate carrots, sweet potatoes, squash, and other yellow vegetables as well.

SHARING YOUR PLATE

Eating is typically a social activity, both for humans and for parrots, so it is very

Young birds have specific nutritional needs. Be certain to consult with your breeder or avian vet before bringing home a young Grey.

common for a pet bird to join its humans at the table. Obviously you won't want to be using the best china and crystal when dining with your Grey, nor would it be the best way to impress your new boss, unless your boss is also a parrot person.

SIZE MATTERS

Your feathered buddy may sit on your shoulder and talk with you, watch television with you, and share your snacks, but a parrot is very different from you in a very important way when it comes to eating—size. If you eat a chip loaded with fat and salt, or even a handful of chips, it isn't the best thing for you, but it won't kill you outright. For your Grey, however, a handful of chips can be extremely unhealthy.

The difference in your sizes is what makes the crucial distinction here. Even if parrots and humans have exactly the same tolerance for various substances, depending on how big you are, a given amount of some substance ingested by your parrot may represent more than 100 times the amount it does to you. The fat or salt content of the chips remains the same, of course, but the amount of fat or salt per body weight is hugely different. So, if you melt half a stick of butter and pour it lavishly over some popcorn, and then split the popcorn with your Grey, you each get 2 ounces of butter. For you, that is probably 0.1 and 0.3 percent of your body weight. For the parrot, it is about 15 to 20 percent— the equivalent of a 150-pound person eating about 25 pounds of butter! So, what

Variety is the spice of life, so give your Grey as many options as possible during mealtimes, but remove fresh fruits and vegetables before they spoil.

seemed like simply sharing a snack is instead a major health concern.

Because the difference between a drug and a poison is one of dosage, you must keep the size differential in mind about common drugs as well. Caffeine, widely used as a stimulant, is fairly safe for human beings; the lethal dose is between 50 and 200 cups of coffee—something no one is likely to ingest. For a bird, however, this drops to less than a cup of coffee—within conceivable consumption levels. Of course, if parrots are more susceptible than we are to caffeine poisoning, the amount would be even less. The same goes for alcohol, which should never be offered to your bird.

Friend or Performer?

With a pet parrot, you have a choice of whether you want just a feathered friend or a trained performer. Of course, your bird can be a pal in either case, but your relationship will necessarily be a bit different if you choose the trainer-performer roles.

ADEPT PERFORMERS

If you have ever seen a good parrot show,

A T stand is a useful tool for training the step up and step down commands.

THE GUIDE TO OWNING AN AFRICAN GREY PARROT

you know that these birds make incredibly talented performers. They are able to sing duets, ride bicycles, do gymnastics, retrieve objects from the audience, and literally fly through hoops on command. It usually appears that the birds are enjoying themselves as well—something I don't often perceive in the case of trained dog or lion acts. To me, the dogs always seem nervously anxious about doing what their masters want them to correctly, and the big cats always seem humiliated and looking for a chance for escape or revenge. But for birds, performing in a show is an interesting and stimulating interaction with the human "flock."

The intelligence and toddler-like perverseness of parrots also manifests itself in these shows. I recall a show in which an Amazon parrot started things off with a dialogue with the human performer. "How are you?" "I'm fine, how are you?" I saw the show several times, but one time the parrot kept asking "How are you?" over and over, eliciting a nervous laugh and an "I'm fine, thanks" from the trainer and appreciative laughter from the crowd. The bird picked up on this, and during the rest of the time, it interjected a quick "How are you?" at every opportunity, ad-libbing to the audience's delight and the human trainer's exasperation—her smile was truly painted on by the end of the act, and you could almost see the one on the parrot.

The tricks that parrots perform can be quite complex. This same show featured a macaw that would take an envelope from the trainer, fly over the crowd to a rural delivery mailbox located high in the open-air amphitheater, open the box, put the envelope inside, close it, raise the red flag, and fly back to the trainer's arm. I have seen a conure that did a Wild West skit, swaggering around with a cowboy hat on and executing a melodramatic dying scene when "shot" with a cap pistol. The list goes on and includes birds that roller-skate backwards, do complicated gymnastic routines, and solve puzzles.

TURNING THE TABLES

Most parrot owners prefer simply to interact informally with their pets. This does not preclude tricks, however; often it is the parrot that dreams up the routine and teaches it to the human.

A typical scenario would be the mischievous parrot doing something that elicits a response from you. The parrot then reacts, then you respond to that. This can lead to a routine that gets repeated and provides amusement for both you and the bird.

Even more common are the numerous "tricks" worked out between the two of you. The bird nibbles your ear, you give it a piece of whatever you're eating. You tap your shoulder, the bird flies to you and lands there. The bird says "Out!" and you open its cage. You pick up a towel and the parrot flies to the shower to wait for you.

A parrot's talent for mimicry is not confined to vocalizations, and your pet will imitate many of your behaviors—or try to! Whether you want to stage your own parrot shows or just enjoy your little Grey friend spontaneously, you will find it an amusing and affectionate pal.

TALKING

If you are planning to buy a Grey so you can teach it to talk, you should forget your plans right now. There is no guarantee that any parrot, even an African Grey, will learn to speak. True, with some species it is the exceptional bird that talks well, but it is a rare Grey who does not. It is, however, an unfair and unreasonable expectation to make

A bird held below eye level will know that you are in charge, which is something to keep in mind before letting your Grey ride around on your shoulder.

of a bird, and if your enjoyment of your pet depends on its talking, you should reconsider. Even if it does learn to speak, that does not mean it will be like Alex (who has had 20 years of intensive training), or that it will be able to astonish your family and friends. Greys vary considerably in speaking ability (or desire?). On the other hand, most Greys will learn to talk. By the time they are weaned a few Greys are already speaking, though most do not speak until they are between a year and two years old.

Can You Teach Your Grey to Talk?

Will a Grey just spontaneously learn to speak? Some do, and even wild-caught birds that are not specifically trained often begin to use human language. Those that perform exceptionally well, however, receive a great deal of training. On the other hand, few Greys receive the formal instruction that Alex has, and yet some Greys exceed even his accomplishments, especially in terms of vocabulary size.

It is clear that to maximize your bird's learning to speak, you should maximize the opportunity and the motivation it has to learn. Parrots often learn when they are observers, and it is common for an eavesdropping bird to learn as well or even better than one that is being actively "taught."

Use speech to communicate with your pet, and reward it when it tries to talk. Make talking fun for your bird—games, puzzles, and new toys are great ways to include new vocabulary words.

THE GUIDE TO OWNING AN AFRICAN GREY PARROT

Short training sessions—whether for commands or talking—can easily be worked into a daily routine.

Dialogue is natural for these animals. A parrot flock stays in close communication nevertheless are always in contact vocally. It is a small step for these natural mimics to use the same sounds you do to have this kind of dialogue. Greys seem to learn their own names and those of other household members (including other pets) very easily, and they use them, so address your bird by name, and refer to yourself with the term you prefer the bird to use for you.

UNLEARNING

A final word of warning: it is impossible to unteach a parrot, so do not teach it to say something you will later regret its being able to say. It is a sad and completely humorless fact that many parrots are destroyed because no one will give them a home due to their filthy vocabularies.

Health Concerns

The range of diseases that can afflict your pet parrot includes some horrible and incurable afflictions—and even a couple that you can also contract. Fortunately,

Greys can live as long as some humans, provided they are healthy and well cared for.

the list of diseases most pet Greys typically succumb to is a whole lot smaller. Though the former is of real concern for a breeder with a room full of birds and constant traffic of animals in and out, the single Grey owner need not worry so much. Rather than concentrate on ailments you are unlikely to face and for which you will need a veterinarian's assistance anyway, let's take a look at the common maladies to affect pet Greys.

NONSTICK COOKWARE

Rightfully at the top of this list is death by nonstick cookware. When the nonstick coating is overheated it produces incredible toxic fumes, to which birds are unfortunately very susceptible. Horror stories abound of birds being killed when an unwatched pot boiled dry. Very often, a minute or two of relaxed caution is all that is needed. Many bird owners refuse to

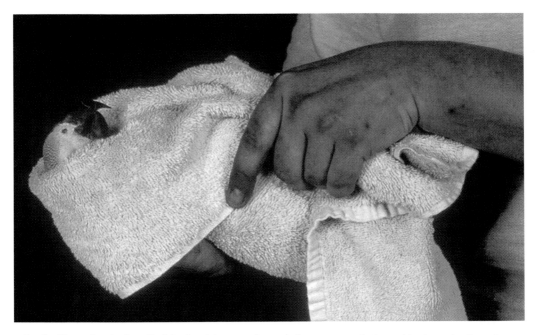

A bird will need to be handled for health procedures such as exams, shots, and tests, so try to get your bird used to being held in a towel.

have any of this material in their kitchens. If you do use nonstick cookware, make sure you follow the manufacturer's instructions to the letter about cooking temperatures, and never leave the room if you are using these utensils. Nonstick coatings and heating elements—a lethal combination—are also found in hair dryers, room heaters, and clothes irons, and parrot deaths have been attributed to their use as well.

OTHER POISONOUS GASES

Do you know about the use of canaries in coal mines? Decades ago miners would carry a caged canary into the mine with them. If they encountered dangerous gas concentrations, the canary would keel over before the miners even experienced any symptoms, and they would have time to evacuate before they dropped. Well, it isn't just canaries that are hypersensitive to deadly fumes, and you can figure that any gas that is dangerous to you is even more lethal for your Grey. In fact, those fumes from nonstick cookware are deadly to humans, too, but in much greater amounts than is necessary to kill a bird. As an illustration, I know of no cases of humans dying from a single overheated pot, but many birds have died this way.

Recently a breeder in Florida had a devastating loss when a delivery truck was left idling in the driveway near an intake for the birdroom's air exchange system. Likewise, even a minor fire often results in the death of any birds in the house due to deadly fumes. Whatever the poison—methane, carbon monoxide, burning plastics, pesticides, or upholstery cleaner—a bird will succumb long before people or other pets.

Feather plucking can be a serious problem for Greys, perhaps because of the high level of frustration they feel when bored or left alone.

HOUSEHOLD POISONS

It is not the obvious poisons like fly sprays, rodent killers, or ant bait that are commonly the cause of death of pet birds, because most owners keep these away from their birds. (Remember that birds are many times more sensitive to these chemicals than we are, and the safest level of pesticide concentration to permit around your bird is zero.) It is the unrecognized toxicity of many common household chemicals that brings about the demise of an unfortunate number of pet parrots. Cleaners, polishes, stain removers, fabric softeners, and many others can be very dangerous.

The problem in putting together a list, however, is that very little is actually known about the safety of these substances. This has led to a situation where rumors run rampant, and well-meaning bird owners quickly spread each and every tale of a bird death due to some product without any type of documentation. This, of course, is erring on the side of caution, something we all want to do with a valued and valuable pet. Even if there weren't new products coming onto the market all the time, it would be impossible to make sure we've included everything in a list of proscribed materials. The safe path to pursue, therefore, is one of extreme caution: *Do not use any chemicals that you do not know to be completely safe on, near, or around your pet bird.*

This becomes an issue mainly when selecting the products used to clean your parrot's cage, dishes, and play area. The old standby of chlorine bleach is a fine choice, provided it is rinsed off thoroughly, but there are many other germicidal cleaners that are manufactured specifically for use in bird cages. Unfortunately a "safe for pets" label on a household cleaner does not mean it is safe to use around your bird. Your pet retailer should have a selection of products for you to choose from, but you should be extremely cautious about using regular cleaning products. Keep in mind, however, that a parrot given free run of the house is more likely to come into contact with products not intended for use around birds.

TOXIC PLANTS

Because parrots are inveterate nibblers and gnawers, they can easily be killed by poisonous household plants. Unfortunately, many commonly kept household plants are quite poisonous, including (but not limited to) poinsettia, Dieffenbachia, ivy, philodendron, and mistletoe. In addition, many common landscaping plants can be deadly, including azalea, wisteria, lily of the valley, and rhododendron. The toxicity of plants can be quite species-specific—I once lost a sheep that died after eating just one rhododendron leaf, but deer eat rhododendron regularly with impunity. Even the vegetable garden is a potential source of poisoning. Tomato and potato leaves are poisonous. Rhubarb leaves and roots contain calcium oxalate, which is extremely dangerous, which is why only the stalks are edible—for you or your parrot.

The best plan here is again one of caution: if you don't know for a fact that a plant is safe for you to eat, don't let your parrot eat it. The only plant that is edible by us but suspect for feeding to birds is avocado. There are reports of avocado being toxic to birds, and there are reports of people feeding their birds avocado with no ill effects. Personally, I won't risk feeding avocado to my birds until and unless I am convinced it is safe. There are plenty of other fruits you can use safely.

PEOPLE POISONS

Most homes contain poisons that humans regularly ingest. Many of these are known or suspected carcinogens, and many others cause other medical problems. These include "recreational poisons" such as tobacco smoke, caffeine, and alcohol, none of which will benefit either you or

Handfeeding a young bird or an ill bird is a difficult process and one that can result in serious harm if done incorrectly.

Nail trimming may be reduced or eliminated altogether by using concrete perches, which wear down nails and prevent excessive growth.

your bird, but all of which you can tolerate in much higher doses than a parrot.

There is also a category we might call "necessary poisons," which includes prescription medications and caustic chemicals such as lye and petroleum distillates. In the same way that all of these substances must be kept from children, they must be kept from your bird. Just remember that the "childproofing" here has to be targeted to your parrot—your flying, climbing, and curious parrot.

Metal Poisoning

Many metals are poisonous to your bird, just as they are to you. The difference is that you are unlikely to go around chewing on metal, but your parrot will, especially if it is soft and malleable.

Lead

Lead is probably the best known poisonous metal, so it is the one most often eliminated in today's homes. Lead paint is only found in old buildings, and lead pipes in older still. Lead solder, however, has only recently been eliminated from home construction, which means if your bird has access to copper plumbing (which it shouldn't unless you enjoy repairing leaks!) it might have access to lead as well.

Mercury

Mercury, another well-known poison, is not a common household metal, but it is found in some thermometers and as a component of certain chemical products. Obviously, you should not allow your bird access to these dangers.

Zinc

Because of its alleged involvement in various physiological processes, zinc is somewhat of a trendy food supplement for humans. It is, however, deadly in anything other than minute amounts, and it is, unfortunately, involved in galvanizing. Homemade cages are usually made with galvanized wire, and zinc deposits on the wire can kill birds when they chew on them. They do not have to eat the metal; just chewing on it can give them a lethal dose.

The way to avoid this is to purchase cages from reputable manufacturers, and if you build your own, to use quality GAW (galvanized after welding) wire, and then to scrub the wire with vinegar, rinse it well, and then allow it to weather outside. Some people ignore this advice and succeed, but others lose their birds to zinc poisoning.

Iron

Because iron is such a vital nutrient, being a major component of blood's hemoglobin, many people do not realize that it can be toxic in very large doses. In parrots this is very rare, and the only time it occurs is when vitamin and mineral supplements are improperly used. A bird cannot normally overdose by chewing on iron. In fact, the safest metal to use around your bird is stainless steel—made from iron.

Aluminum

The toxicity of aluminum is much under debate, with alarmists at one end claiming it's a brain-cell-destroying menace in any amount and naysayers on the other saying it's perfectly safe. As usual, the truth is undoubtedly in the middle somewhere. There is no question, however, that aluminum's soft nature makes it an easy target for a parrot's powerful bill. This means that at the best it will be quickly destroyed, and it would not be good for your bird if it ingested the metal.

It's fairly simple to create homemade toys for your Grey, but be absolutely certain that the materials are safe and non-toxic.

An older bird may require special considerations, perhaps a soft rope perch or platform for sore feet.

GET A VET!

The symptoms of disease in a parrot include ruffled feathers, lethargy, loss of appetite, off-color or runny stools, nasal discharge, and general droopiness. The problem is, these are symptoms of just about all bird ailments. Even talking Greys cannot tell you how they feel. This means that direct examination and laboratory tests are the only way to diagnose your bird's illness, and this means that you need a reliable avian veterinarian.

The time to find this doctor is before you even acquire your pet. Then, before you bring your Grey home, it should visit its new doctor. The vet can make sure your bird is healthy and get some baseline vital statistics against which the bird can be compared if it becomes ill. In addition, you and the doctor can discuss health concerns, emergency contact instructions, and other issues important to both of you.

Because a sick bird is the first one to be picked off by a predator, birds will not show signs of illness until they are really feeling poorly, and they can go downhill very rapidly after that. Waste no time in getting your bird to the vet. Birds respond very well to many medical treatments, provided they are administered in time. And, if your bird does not need any treatment, that peace of mind is well worth the visit.

Breeding Greys

Breeding parrots are not pets. This is not to say that pet parrots cannot be bred, but while they are nesting, they rarely still behave as pets. In addition, a mated pair of birds will usually have a stronger bond between them than they will have with humans. Aside from this fact, however, breeding your bird is not something you should contemplate doing until you have a great deal of experience. However, you may at some future time wish to consider making this step, so I will quickly outline the basics here. Remember, though, that being a tame pet is not an asset in the breeding situation, and the vast majority of breeding Greys in captivity are not tame pets.

MATE SELECTION

Some people start with a mated pair. This is usually successful, because Greys are typically gentle and faithful mates, and the spouse attacks that plague some other large parrot pairs are very rare with a Grey pair. As with people, there is no telling which two birds will form a permanent bond, and there are pairs with one wild-caught member, one hand-tame member, and all other possible variations. Most breeding pairs are in the 10- to 20-year-old range, though there are younger and older breeders around.

Another way to get started is to buy a group of younger birds and let them pair up in a large flight cage or aviary. The first few pairs are generally stable, but as the pickings get slimmer, some birds may have to settle for what's left, and the pairing might not be so compatible. Thus, even with equal numbers of each sex, you may get fewer pairs than half the number of birds.

The least successful way to get a pair is simply to acquire a male and a female and hope for the best. They can wind up enemies, just friends, or a pair, but there is no way to predict.

Different styles of nest boxes are available; it may take some trial and error before you find what works best for you and your birds.

ACCOMMODATIONS

Breeding Greys need a private, spacious cage or flight. They often will not go to nest if kept near other parrots, especially noisy ones like cockatoos, and while the calls of other pairs of Greys can facilitate breeding, it is best if the cages are isolated visually so that the birds do not spend their time and energy "fighting" through the bars.

The perches in the cage must be firmly attached so that the birds will have a secure place to copulate successfully. There should be toys in the cage as well, but because the bulk of the birds' time will be spent caring for the eggs and chicks, you do not need an elaborate play gym in there.

Different breeders have different success with various designs of nest boxes. Many use a grandfather clock nest, which is tall and narrow, with a wire mesh ladder to assist the birds in climbing to the entrance hole at the top. Others use boot boxes or other adaptations—L-shapes and other designs that provide separate areas within the box. The box is filled with shavings, which the birds remove to the depth they want; this mimics their natural behavior of excavating or renovating holes in rotten trees This behavior also helps prevent clear (infertile) eggs. How?

The hen is stimulated to lay eggs by the presence of a suitable nesting cavity, but it takes a couple of weeks or more for an egg to develop. Because fertilization must take place early in this process—after yolk formation but before the white and shell are added—if the female finds a nest ready

One way to set up breeding pairs is to let the birds choose their mates themselves. Keep in mind that most breeders will be between 10 and 20 years old.

THE GUIDE TO OWNING AN AFRICAN GREY PARROT

to move into, she may start to produce eggs before mating has even taken place. Thus, nest building serves also to ensure egg fertility! In fact, sometimes breeders with overeager pairs have success after covering the holes of the nest boxes with thin wood to make it take longer for the birds to prepare the nest.

FEEDING

Needless to say, birds must be in prime condition before breeding, or the physical strain will dangerously lower their reserves and resistance to disease. This applies to both parents, because as monogamous breeders they share the nutritional burden of raising young quite equitably.

Although it is obviously the female alone that contributes the nutrients in the eggs, the male balances this by feeding the female while she is incubating the eggs. Once the eggs hatch, both parents become full-time feeding machines, unless you pull the chicks to hand raise them, in which case you become a full-time feeding machine.

The birds' normal diet should be fine for breeding, too, with a greater emphasis on protein and minerals to supply the needs of the rapidly growing chicks. Fruits and vegetables are still important for the vitamins they contain, but you don't want your birds filling up on these low-protein foods; they should be reduced and high-protein soft foods should be increased. One of the best supplements is eggs.

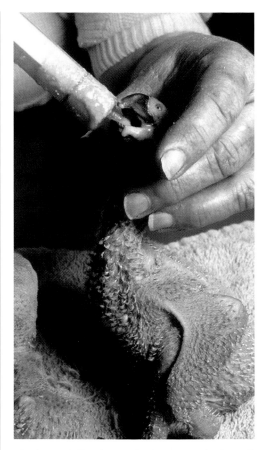

Think carefully about whether your chicks will be parent-raised or handfed. Handfeeding is a serious time commitment that involves around-the-clock feedings.

If you think about it, a chicken egg (with shell) is just about the ideal food for birds, because it contains everything needed to make a whole new bird! And most birds love crushed, whole hard-boiled eggs, and they eagerly feed them to their young.

RAISING CHICKS

Although many pairs will feed their chicks right up to weaning, most babies are taken from the nest early and handraised. This process is well beyond the scope of this book, and it is not something you can learn by reading about it in any case. If you want

The rewards of breeding are well worth the time and effort—more healthy, young African Greys!

to go into breeding Greys, you will need to study under an experienced breeder to learn this and the other procedures necessary for success.

Remember, this chapter has not been a guide to breeding parrots, only an introduction to the topics you will need to learn about if you wish to pursue this course. First take time to get to know Greys, and your own Grey in particular. Very few Grey owners go on to become breeders, but almost every single Grey owner does go on to have a lifetime bond with a very special feathered friend. Good luck!

Index

Index

Photo Credits